IMAGES OF
Rochdale

IMAGES OF Rochdale

ROCHDALE
METROPOLITAN BOROUGH
COUNCIL

ROCHDALE
OBSERVER

Compiled by
Richard Catlow and John Cole

The Breedon Books
Publishing Company
Derby

First published in Great Britain by
The Breedon Books Publishing Company Limited
Breedon House, 44 Friar Gate, Derby, DE1 1DA.
1996

ISBN 1 85983 056 0

Printed and bound by Butler & Tanner Ltd., Selwood Printing
Works, Caxton Road, Frome, Somerset.

Colour separations by Colour Services, Wigston, Leicester.

Jackets printed by Lawrence-Allen, Weston-super-Mare, Avon.

Contents

Introduction 7

A Stroll Through Rochdale Centre 8

Out And About 40

Rochdale At Work 43

Getting About 64

The Best Days Of Our Life! 87

Then And Now 90

Sport And Leisure 95

The Weighvers' Seaport 112

So Many Things To Do 115

Personalities And Celebrities 122

Visitors 131

Celebrations 133

Processions 141

Churches 144

War And Remembrance 148

Doom And Disaster 155

Local Services 163

Around The District 171

Acknowledgements

Although many of the photographs in this book have come from the files of the *Rochdale Observer*, this publication could not have been compiled without the help of hundreds of local people. We have tried to acknowledge as many as possible, particularly those who answered an appeal for pictures in the *Rochdale Observer* or donors to the Local History Collection at the library. To those we have missed, our apologies.

Particular thanks must go to John and Eric Bollington whose knowledge of local railways was an invaluable help, to Harry O'Neill who has spent years building up a fine collection of local photographs, to members of the Whitworth Museum and to Neil Caygill who put us on the right track for several interesting pictures and stories.

Our main thanks go, however, to a remarkable man without whose life's work Rochdale would be a poorer place indeed. Clifford C.Ashton chronicled life in the town for decades a speciality (as readers will see) was in capturing the frequent blazes which destroyed several cotton mills locally. But, as a freelance photographer working for the *Observer* and other papers, he was present at innumerable events. His help has been invaluable.

Introduction

AS ONE of the oldest towns in Lancashire, Rochdale has experienced more changes over the centuries than most of its neighbours.

Developing slowly from its Anglo-Saxon origins, into an eighteenth-century market and woollen producing centre, Rochdale was transformed by the Industrial Revolution into a powerhouse of textile manufacture. Between 1820 and 1880 the population of the borough quadrupled, factory chimneys erupted over the skyline and the town spread outwards along its arterial highways.

Architecturally, the town became a kaleidoscope of differing styles. Victorian Rochdale experienced a frenzy of building ranging from the magnificent to the monstrous. Whilst the Town Hall occupied a vast area adjacent to the River Roch, working-class houses were crushed together, as many as possible squeezed into every available plot, producing dwellings of surreally impractical shapes and almost unimaginable squalor.

Historic buildings in the town centre were swept away. The last surviving Tudor timber-beamed house on Yorkshire Street was unceremoniously flattened in 1890. Summercastle House, with its adjacent windmill had disappeared 40 years earlier.

However, the street patterns remained the same. Yorkshire Street branched at the bottom market to Lord Street, Toad Lane and Blackwater Street. Toad Lane itself stretched from the town centre to Heights Lane and via the Turnpike to Whitworth.

Only in the last 40 years have parts of Rochdale been totally obliterated as the needs of the car and changing shopping patterns ruthlessly dictated the shape of the town centre.

Blackwater Street, Lord Street, the Old Clock Face and the top and bottom markets have gone forever and Toad Lane, dissected by the expanded St Mary's gate is forlornly stranded on the wrong side of the Yorkshire Street Shopping Centre. Whilst many of the photographs in this book vividly depict the changes that have taken place, they also serve to illustrate how vital it is to cherish and preserve the best of what remains. This includes not only the grander buildings such as St Chad's Parish Church and the Town Hall, but also the remaining ginnels and alleyways around the Butts, the weavers' cottages on the top of Drake Street and the fine row of buildings which comprise South Parade.

Rochdale still possesses one of the most attractive town centres in the North, (largely due to the impracticality of building on the river covering) but probably could not sustain the loss of many more quality buildings without surrendering what remains of its special character.

What applies to Rochdale applies in equal measure to the surrounding townships and villages. Contained within these pages are photographic memories of the changing faces of Littleborough, Milnrow, Wardle, Whitworth and other areas formerly comprising the Ancient Parish of Rochdale.

However, this book is not only about architecture it is also about people. Many of these photographs feature scenes which are just around the corner of our memories. Yes, our surroundings have altered, yes so have we and yet… and yet it's all there, the way we were the day before yesterday. From pubs and clubs, buses and trams (the first time round), to sport and the theatre, from the mundane to the extraordinary, the images reflect and capture life not so long ago in over 350 *Images of Rochdale*.

Richard Catlow
John Cole

A Stroll Through Rochdale Centre

From the air... the town centre in 1990, virtually a mill-free zone.

Before the huge changes of the 1960s; looking down Manchester Road. The Theatre Hotel is on the right and Holland Street Mill on the left.

One of the oldest photographs of the town. Taken around 1850, it shows Manchester Road with the Holland Street Mill on the right and Castle Hill in the distance.

The same view as the previous photograph in the late 1960s.

The famous 'Angel' on Manchester Road at the foot of Broadfield Park. A memorial to Augusta McKinnon, presented to the town by her daughter Ellen in 1899, it became a famous meeting place for courting couples. A double decker drinking trough beneath the statue provided refreshment for both dogs and horses. Subjected to decades of traffic vibration, the Angel was removed to Entwisle Road transport depot where it eventually disintegrated, or ascended or just plain disappeared.

Taken as recently as 1978, the view over Broadfield Park towards the Trinity Chapel (now demolished) shows how rapidly the area has altered.

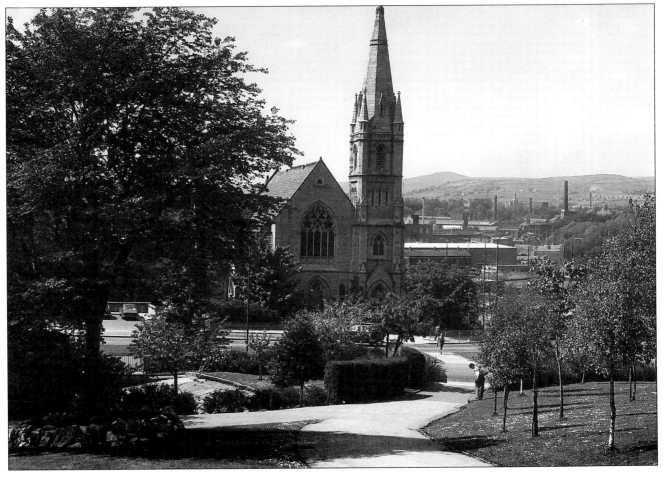

Cows in front of the Town Hall? The Cattle Fairground on Theatre Street was opened in 1877. This view of the Holme, on Town Meadows, dates from 1908.

The Holme was still used as a fairground until the late 1960s. This view, from 1965, shows the first phase of the Art College adjacent to Holland Street Mill and the police courts on the right-hand side.

Above: The avenue of trees which then flanked the Esplanade, looking towards Trinity Chapel, in 1962.

Right, top: The view from the same vantage point as the photograph below. Taken in the 1950s it shows the Memorial Gardens on the site of the Orchard. The Cenotaph, designed by Sir Edwin Lutyens, was completed in 1922.

Right, bottom: The rear of the Memorial Gardens in 1962 showing the junction of Lord Street and Blackwater Street. Hardly a building remains today. (John Sandiford)

A little further down the Esplanade, the 'Manor House' or more correctly the 'Orchard', was home of the Dearden family who purchased the Manor of Rochdale from the poet Byron in 1823. The Orchard was demolished in 1922.

The Memorial Gardens with the Town Centre flats under construction in 1965, taken from the front of the Town Hall. (H.Milne)

In all its original glory. Rochdale Town Hall, 'the finest in the North of England', with its original wooden spire, just after completion in 1871.

The building of the Alfred Waterhouse designed tower in 1886, replacing the original spire which was destroyed by fire three years earlier.

Behind the Town Hall stood Kershaw's Central Corn Mill, the demolition of which in 1934 released 'a plague of terrified rats'.

And before the Town Hall was built... the 'House in the Wood', visited by John Ruskin and photographed here in or around 1860.

The Town Hall from the town centre flats in the late 1960s. The Hippodrome Theatre is behind the Post Office on the left.

The old and the new. The Town Hall and the town centre flats in the 1970s.

This evocative study shows the Town Hall from the top of the 122 Church Steps in or around 1890.

The Top of the Town. Church Stile in the 1890s. The stocks are beneath the arch on the far left.

Before the river covering. The Newgate area, prior to the construction of the street itself in 1895. The present Pioneers store is in the background.

'A river runs through it'. Possibly dating from as early as 1855, this view shows the Wellington Hotel and Drake Street with the lamp post in the middle of the road commemorating the Rochdale Pioneers.

A similar view to the previous photograph, just over a hundred years later in 1961.

The River Roch before covering, in or around 1900. The structure on the left is an omnibus shelter.

A familiar sight, the town centre in turmoil due to work on the river covering. This was taken during the latter stages of the creation of 'the widest bridge in the world' in 1924.

The catacombs of Rochdale. The bed of the river which had been covered in 1903, showing columns, beams and old plate girders.

The covering needed to be immensely strong to withstand the weight and vibration of the local tramway network.

Butts House, Kelsall and Kemps Butts Mill, the Bowling Green and Duncan Street Mills in 1928.

By 1961, Butts House and ancillary buildings had been replaced by the Regal Cinema. The demolition of Kelsall and Kemps mill began the following year. (John Sandiford)

By the time demolition of the mill began in 1962 the Regal had become the ABC.

In 1962 the cleared site (now occupied by the municipal offices) reveals Hardman's Mill in the background.

On the Butts itself, the original Royds (Yes, ROYDS the Rochdale bankers) building. In the 1970s it had become the SELNEC transport office.

The same view as the previous photograph with William Deacons using the premises in 1909. The building on the right, before its chocolate box façade was added, now houses the Royal Bank of Scotland.

Smith Street, with Electric House on the right and the Yelloway Bus Depot on the left, alongside the Town Weir on the Roch.

Back to the future? Tram lines were first laid in Drake Street in 1904. Now there are plans to run the Metrolink tram service down the street.

Drake Street with Fashion Corner and the Star Hotel on the left in 1955.

Just a little further up Drake Street on the same day with the Norma Café on the right, which later became the town's first Chinese restaurant.

The then bustling Drake Street pictured ten years later in October 1965.

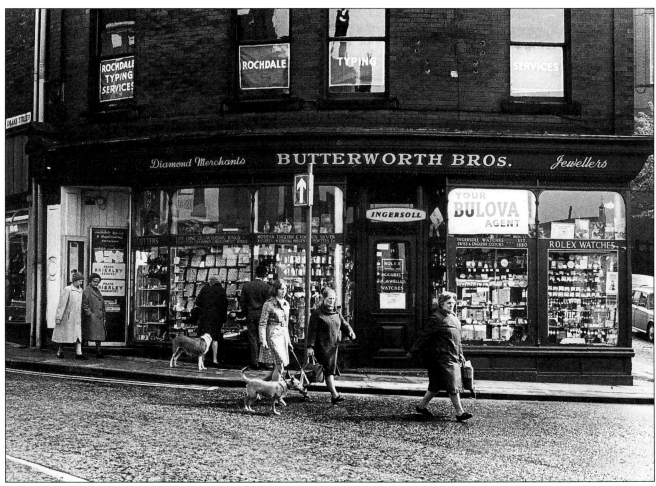

Butterworth's the jewellers have traded on Drake Street since 1880. This view dates from May 1969.

Before the shopping precinct. Lord Street meets Newgate with the Hippodrome Theatre on the right and the Pioneers (formerly the Provident) Co-operative stores behind the Red Lion.

And now on to Yorkshire Street on a decidedly damp day in July 1970.

Again gone, but certainly not forgotten. This view was taken in 1959, looking back up Newgate to Blackwater Street with the Hippodrome on the left. (K.George)

But the sun does shine on Yorkshire Street. This view dates from 1955. On the right we have Yates' Wine Lodge, the Bon-Bon Café and the Yorkshire Penny Bank. (H.Milne)

The bottom of Yorkshire Street, looking up towards Seniors (still with us) and the market and showing the justifiably famous 'Jimmy Duck's' (James Duckworth's) grocers in 1925.

The same view exactly 30 years later.

Two-way traffic on upper Yorkshire Street in or around 1930.

A similar view to the previous photograph showing the Reed Hotel entry, on the right, in about 1945.

Before the Whitworth Road roundabout. The junction of Whitworth Road and Yorkshire Street, at the top of John Street, in 1956. (B.R.Barrass)

Looking down Whitworth Road, again to St John's Church, in the same year as the previous photograph.

The changes begin. The town centre redevelopment in the mid-1970s. The old market is shown, top left.

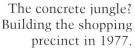

The concrete jungle?
Building the shopping
precinct in 1977.

Totally unrecognisable
now, Cheetham Street
in 1963, looking
towards the Spotland
Road junction of Bury
Road. (John Sandiford)

And equally unrecognisable, St Mary's Gate in 1961 before it dissected the town as a dual carriageway. In the distance is the Pioneer's Central Stores. (Leonard Russell)

Formerly one of the longest streets in Rochdale, Toad Lane, the home of the Pioneers, in 1890.

Meanwhile, in what was an interesting network of roads and alleyways, Cloth Hall on College Street, the home of the Association of Weavers, Winders and Doublers.

When markets were markets. Rochdale Market Hall in 1900.

When Rochdale had an open market. The old Fish Market in 1900 with Irlam's tripe dressers behind and the Woolpack Hotel in the distance.

The Open Market, bustling with shoppers, after the Wakes holidays in August 1962.

A new section of the outdoor market opened in Toad Lane in summer 1962.

Looking like something off a film set, the outside market on Toad Lane and the Old Clock Face Hotel in 1895.

Fast forward to 1970 and the Old Clock Face with the Town Flats rearing up in the background. Eight years later the Clock Face was also demolished.

Out And About

To Meanwood Brow, Spotland Bridge around 1910. Albert Schofield's newsagents is on the right. The shop with blinds was Adshead's Bakers and Confectioners. The doctor's surgery on the left of the picture is now the After Eight restaurant. (Ken and Ivy Edmondson)

Bygone trades... John Wild's clog shop on Princess Street in the late 1940s. (Clifford C.Ashton)

Weavers' cottages, with their well-lit upper floors where hand-loom weavers worked. Unusually for Rochdale, these on Coldwell Brow, Spotland Road (photographed in 1963) were built of brick not stone. (H.Milne)

Creeping suburbia – looking towards the Cemetery on Bury Road in the 1920s.

Why it's called Sandy Lane. Before and after the road widening between 1928 and 1932.

Major demolition works in the Freehold area in September 1959.

Rochdale At Work

This series of photographs provides an insight into Rochdale's contribution to the nation's wealth when 'Britain's bread hung by Lancashire's thread'. Firstly, however, there was and still is agriculture. This view shows haymaking in rural Bamford in 1959.

More typical of local industry, this aerial view taken in 1923, features part of Wardleworth – including Cheetham Street and High Street mills, terraces, more mills, more terraces.

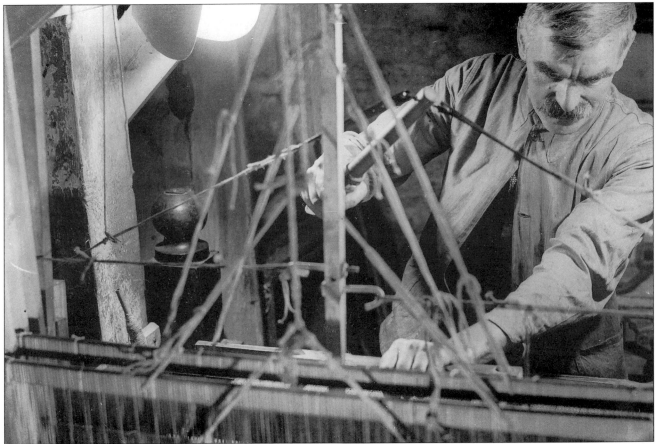

Traditional textile crafts. This photograph is of Mr S.Fielden on a handloom 'built from odds and ends' weaving high grade sheets in November 1935. (Clifford C.Ashton)

Built when cotton was King, a product of the post-World War One building boom, State Mill pictured here in 1984.

The Clovelly Street and Kingsland Road area with the Mars Mill complex in June 1934.

'The mills, work, dominated your life. It was sleep, work, eat, work, drink, work.' It couldn't have done much for your washing either! Local millscape in the 1930s.

A drawing of the massive Clod Mill site in 1908. By diversifying into asbestos from their original business of traditional textiles, Rochdale's Turner Brothers made their fortune.

An aerial view of the same site in the late 1960s, 'the largest asbestos textile factory in the world'. Many of the fields in the background are now covered by housing. The old Rochdale to Bacup rail line, although it had closed many years previously, can still be clearly seen.

'Stretching into infinity'. The number three shed at the Turner Brothers' complex contained 1,500 looms when this photograph was taken in 1920. High-class materials for the colour trade shirtings, dress materials and checks were made here.

Half-timers engaged in roving, possibly at Mitchell Hey Mill in 1900.

The weaving sheds, again possibly at Mitchell Hey, in 1900.

Dunlop Cotton Mills, the world's largest single site mill complex in 1937. The picture shows the number five weaving shed decorated for the coronation of King George VI and Queen Elizabeth.

Away from the clatter of machinery, roller coverers working in the Lodge at Crest Mill, Queensway, in the mid-1940s. (Hannah Haynes)

And a welcome brew. Tea break at the Clover Mill in 1948.

Balderstone mill girls outside the factory in 1962.

Back inside the mills the next photographs show just some of the complexity of machinery and processes at local mills. Depicted above is cotton waste spinning at Passmonds Mill in 1983.

Automatic pirn winding machine at Dunlop Mills in the 1960s.

The Quality Control Room at Moss Mill in the early 1960s.

A quality control inspection takes place at Moss Mill.

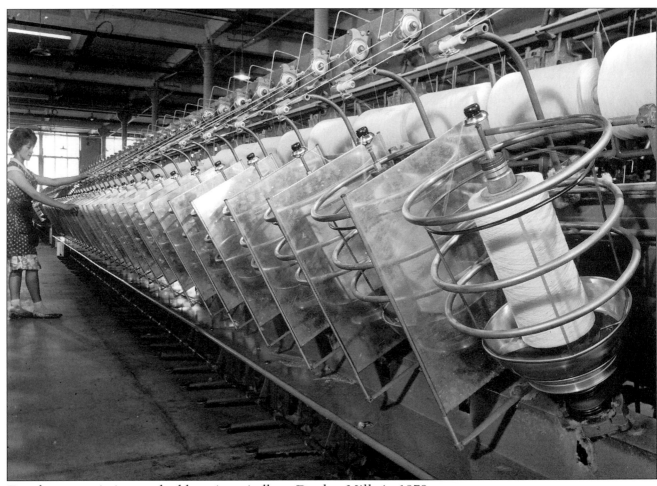

Two-for-one twisting on double twist spindle at Dunlop Mills in 1970.

Installing new plant at Coral Mill in 1963.

Cotton reigned supreme for over a century, fuelling Britain's expansion. We were the workshop of the world. And then, with bewildering speed, in half a generation it was gone. Factories which had powered a revolution were demolished and chimneys which had dominated the landscape were toppled.

The chimney at Millgate works, Smallbridge, going down.

Wool and cotton may have provided the momentum for rapid industrialisation, but there were many other industries, trades and crafts which flourished locally; some like engineering and mining in direct support of the textile sector. Engineering was a major contributor to the economy and James Holroyd and Co. Ltd, machine tool manufacturers of Milnrow, were one of the largest companies. This photograph dates from 1965.

At David Bridge's Castleton factory, an inspection in 1964 of the Watson Stillman aluminium extrusion press.

Locally, coal mining was extensive, providing fuel for the steam-powered mills. Despite the fact that many mines were small drift mines or 'breast highs' driven into hillsides, Butterworth Hall Colliery at Milnrow (pictured here in 1905) was an extremely large concern with shafts and galleries spreading tentacle-like under much of the town.

Neither did all the local pits close before World War Two. Pictured here, in the late 1940s, is the Bamford Close Colliery at Red Lumb.

Pictured here is a Mr A.Whitworth at work on the coal face of the privately-owned Lobden Colliery in October 1949.

Looking towards Littleborough, the Ashworth Clay Works and Starring Potteries in the 1920s with the stock yard on the right and the mined clay being tipped on the dump to the left.

Not usually considered 'woman's work', this rare photograph shows women chainmakers in Milnrow in the 1890s.

With scant regard for the environment, tallow and candles were produced in the centre of Rochdale, under the shadow of the Town Hall, in the 1890s.

The clatter of clogs. Joe Howarth (also known as Joe Clogger) in his shop at 122 Ramsden Road, Wardle, in 1900.

And John Wild, clogger of Princess Street, Rochdale, at work some 50 years later. (Clifford C.Ashton)

Services and supply industries flourished. Whittles bread wholesalers of Littleborough operated from the 1890s until 1957. This photograph shows a delivery van in 1915.

MAPLETON'S COUNTRY WORKS.

(Lithographed from an oil painting.)

Situated 3½ miles from Rochdale at the foot of the moors. 600ft. above sea level.

MAPLETON'S
NUT FOODS

are made from the purest products of sun and air —Nuts and Fruit—and are manufactured under equally ideal conditions. Believing that "Health Foods" cannot be manufactured among city smoke, we have at great expense established ourselves among the green meadows, where mountain and moor, stream and sunshine, lend sweetness to the air.

All orders should be sent direct to the works:

Mapleton's Nut Food Co. Ltd.,
WARDLE, Nr. ROCHDALE.

Descriptive List free on application.

And there's nothing new under the sun. Mapleton's Wholefood Manufacturers operated out of Wardle 'where mountain and moorland lend sweetness to the air' in the early 1900s.

It's claimed that Henry Nuttall's of Rochdale (still in existence today) was the first chip range manufacturer in the world. Be that as it may, most local 'chippies', Hanson's above included, used Nuttall's products.

More recently, Watts' Supper Bar at 18 Smith Street provided service with a smile.

Here, pictured in 1935, is Wardleworth Post Office which was run by the Lord family almost without alteration from the 1920s to the 1980s.

Fizzy pop was big business in Rochdale. Exported worldwide, Casson's soda water was first produced in 1831 and the company flourished independently until 1965 when the CWS bought them for their liquor license. Until recently nearly all CWS wines and spirits were registered under Casson's name. This photograph shows the firm at the height of its success in the 1920s.

An early entry into the recorded music market were A.E.Stott's of Rochdale. Their stand at the 1921 Trade Exhibition at the Territorial Army Hall displayed '78s' and state of the art equipment from Gilbert, HMV and Marconi. (Mrs L.Keegan)

The *Rochdale Observer*, established in 1856, has had many competitors, the *Rochdale Sentinel*, *Times*, *Star* and *Recorder* amongst them, but outlasted them all. The presses are about to roll in this shot taken to mark the paper's centenary.

Getting About

From William Robertson's *Rochdale and the Vale of Whitworth.* 'The last of the lime gal drivers in the Rochdale District was Mary Alice Hartley, more familiarly known as Ailse o' Fussers. In her palmy days she had as many as 20 gals (Galloway ponies) and they carried bags of coal from Land Coalpit near Shawforth and sometimes lime from Clitheroe and Burnley. They travelled the packhorse roads from Cliviger to Bacup along the foot of Brown Wardle, down Cronkeyshaw into Rochdale.' The photograph dates from 1877.

'They shall not pass!' These ladies make a formidable sight as they pose outside the toll bar at Thornham in the 1890s. The turnpike roads, paid for by tolls, vastly improved road transport.

This was the way to get around if you could afford it. Littleborough's Dr McGill on his rounds in horse and trap in around 1900.

The old Rochdale-Norden horse bus.

Roberts' horse omnibus about to set off from the Spread Eagle on Cheetham Street on the Rochdale to Bacup run in 1900.

The charabanc outing was a great adventure. Above, the staff and customers from the Packhorse Hotel in Southport in 1910.

The transport system of the future arrived in Rochdale in the 1880s. Those 'snorting, snarling steam trams' began operating locally in 1883. The original open-top trailers, the pride and joy of the Rochdale, Bury and Oldham Steam Tramway Company, allowed people in the early days to leap to safety if, as occasionally happened, the unreliable beasts lost traction on the inclines and slid backwards causing 'some panic and great hilarity'.

The steam trams were dubbed the 'Baltic Fleet', because like the Czar of Russia's navy they were smoky and unreliable. Here are the wrecking crew at the Mellor Street depot.

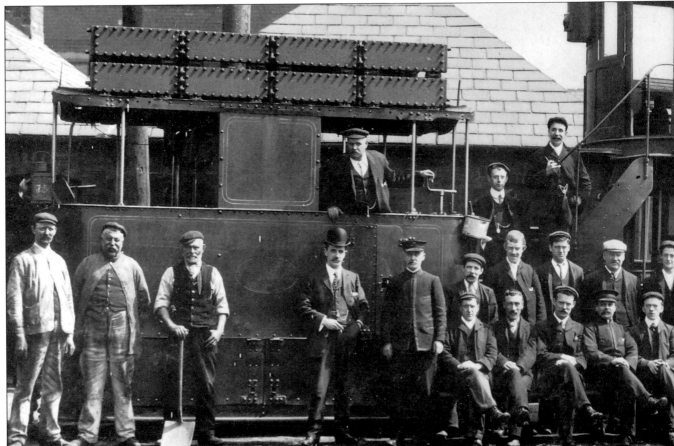

The tram shelter on Broadway, Rochdale town centre, in 1900.

The operating rights were acquired by Rochdale Council and by 1902 the new electric trams were operating on the Bury route. The last steam tram to leave Rochdale is pictured in Littleborough in 1905.

Here is the first electric tram to reach Littleborough in 1905.

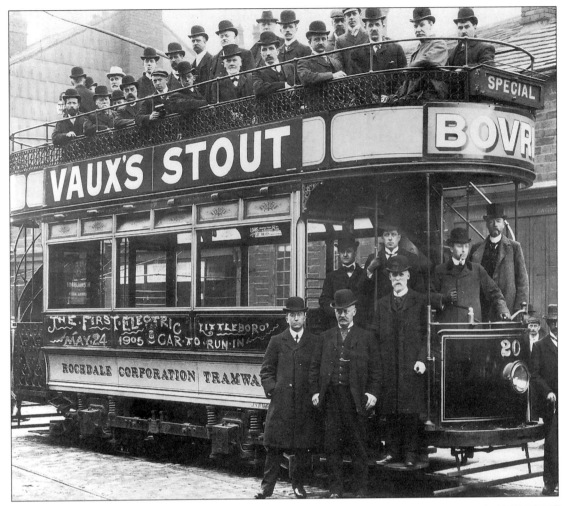

Rochdale town centre with a Thornham-bound tram in around 1920.

The corporation tramway's water sprinkler in 1904. (Harry O'Neill)

The trams may return, the canal is being restored. What next? Packhorses! Here the canal is pictured in the grip of winter at Slattocks in 1905.

Local Rechabites enjoy a canal outing.

Another outing at Healy Bridge in 1907. (Harry O'Neill)

The Rochdale Canal eventually closed to commercial traffic and was allowed to deteriorate and silt up. Here the section at Oldham Road Bridge is getting lots of attention in 1977 when the Cleaning Project made a major environmental impact.

Built to carry stone from the quarries in the Whitworth area to Rochdale; the Rochdale to Bacup line was opened in 1870. Here a passenger train crosses the magnificent Healey Dell viaduct. Passenger services ended on 16 June 1947.

Thundering under Clegg Hall Bridge at Smithy Bridge is a Fowler 7F goods engine heading towards Rochdale in the inter-war years. (John C.Wild)

A runaway train from Rochdale branch sidings in March 1965, came to grief just short of the Roch Valley Viaduct on Entwistle Road. The engine is a Class 8 freight.

A Lancashire and Yorkshire Railway Aspinall 440 tender engine in the early 1900s travelling towards Manchester. The Fothergill and Harvey works near Summit, Littleborough, have altered little over the years.

Rochdale's second railway station was at Wardleworth. The sign to it can be seen behind the two gentlemen with the white horse.

Rochdale's original railway station opened in 1842. A new station complex was opened in April 1889. In 1979, Rochdale's six platforms were reduced to three and the station completely re-designed. The photograph shows holidaymakers off for the Wakes Weeks holidays.

Returning in rain hats from the Wakes holiday in August 1960.

The age of steam revisited. A Roch Valley Railway Society excursion to Facit photographed near Gale Street in August 1962. The engine is a Lancashire & Yorkshire Railway A Class.

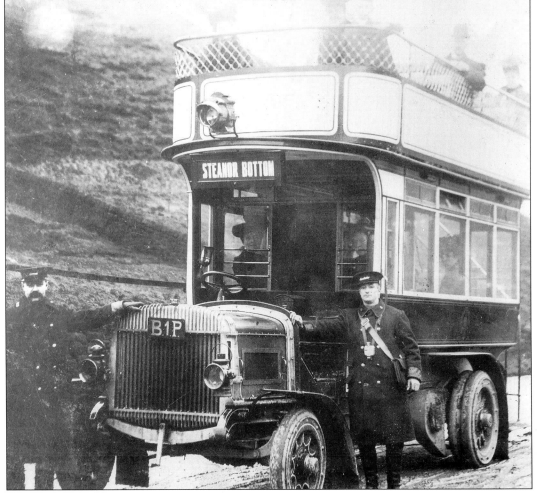

Motor buses made their appearance on routes where there was no tram. Here a pre-World War One motor omnibus, linking Rochdale and Todmorden, pauses for a quick photo-opportunity at Steanor Bottom.

In solitary splendour outside Rochdale Town Hall, is the Number 9 Ashton/Oldham bus in the mid-1940s.

Showing off the famous blue and white livery is Number 1 on the Castleton ro⌄
in 1969. (Roy Marshall)

A mayoral inspection of the Mellor Street Bus Depot in April 1964.

...amatic picture shows an argument between a private coach and a lamp-post on Manchester Road, ...n, in the 1950s.

Ploughing on to Blackpool through heavy snow drifts at Red Lumb in January 1962.

A Yelloways 'chara outing' for Smallbridge pensioners in June 1960.

A David Bridge children's trip catered for by Ellen Smith in January 1963.

And so to the joys of the open road. This was possibly the first car in Rochdale, owned by a Mr Samuel Underwood, seen here fiercely proud with his daughter Sarah up front.

The eleventh car to be registered in Rochdale (the town's number plate letters were DK) was owned by the Hayes family of Wardle.

Taking the invitation literally, an Austin A40 inspects the kitchens on Oldham Road in April 1964. (Clifford C.Ashton)

Snow creates havoc
and a tanker slithers
down an incline in
Norden in February
1963.

A beer lorry makes an unscheduled stop at a grocer's shop in Halifax Road in May 1962.

Gleaming chrome and paintwork. Ford Zephyrs and Zodiacs on display at Rochdale Motor Garage in July 1960.

More traffic, more roads. Here, in September 1924, local dignitaries (and helpers) perform their civic duties for the opening of Queensway.

The building of the M62 motorway was an enormous undertaking, especially the section over the Pennines. Here the Rakewood Viaduct, above Hollingworth Lake, is under construction in 1967. (Clifford C.Ashton)

A closer view of the work on the giant pillars. (Clifford C.Ashton)

The 'all weather motorway' completed. An aerial picture from 1970 shows the Milnrow Interchange, with Butterworth Hall Mill in the distance and Ellenroad Mill on the right.

The Best Days Of Our Life!

The following series of photographs show the changing lives of local people, beginning with the happiest days of your life (you mean that's as good as it gets?) in school. Pictured above is the Rochdale Technical School (later Broadfield School) in 1900. The building has been replaced by an oblong box and a car park.

The laundry class in the Technical School in 1901 when the teacher was Miss Stanley and the course embraced instruction in the best method of washing, starching and ironing.

Children at drill (boys and girls segregated of course) in Balderstone, St Mary's School in about 1920.

Pupils make an impressive sight at the Girls' Grammar School speech day in April 1962. But who is missing from the front row and why? Was she receiving a prize?

Champness Hall again for the Technical School speech day in December 1961.

Old mill, new school. With Moss Mill in the background, pupils at St Peter's School at play in September 1961.

Then And Now

Contrasting lifestyles. After our series of urban landscapes, the tranquillity of Ashworth Fold in or around 1860.

Edward and Hannah Fitton celebrating their golden wedding in 1895.

The almost regal splendour of the dining room at Healey Hall in 1920.

A contrast in living standards. The Milkstone Road area in 1947.

The Milkstone area in 1947.

It seemed like a good idea at the time. The Ashfield Valley flats in 1968. Thirty years after they were built, nearly all the flats have been demolished.

All, or nearly all, smiles in Rathbone Street in 1910.

A bygone era. These weavers' cottages in High Street, opposite Providence Church, were demolished in March 1939.

Also gone are the terraces on Macmillan Street, seen here framing the art gallery and Town Hall in 1978.

It may look like a famous TV 'soap', but it's actually Entwisle Road from the railway embankment in 1972; on a Monday judging by the washing.

Sport And Leisure

Sport and leisure provided the antidote to the working week. Here we look at a number of leisure pursuits enjoyed by local people. Here at the Smith Street Youth Centre, formerly Rochdale's first swimming baths, the table tennis tables are clearly in great demand.

Go for it! The start of the Hollingworth Lake Relay in 1960.

Under the eccentric patronage of local tycoon Jimmy White, Rochdale Cricket Club enjoyed immense success in the 1920s topping the Central Lancashire League from 1922 to 1925 inclusive and again in 1927. This is the double-winning side of 1922 which also picked up the Wood Cup.

Above: Sporting events attracted enormous crowds, as this view of Littleborough Cricket Club in the late 1940s demonstrates.

Rain stopped play! St John's cricket field submerged in 1902.

'Poor man's golf'. A Knur and Spel event at the Rochdale Police Sports Day at Rochdale Cricket Club, Dane Street, in 1951. The object of this formerly extremely popular game was to whack a small piece of pot (the spel) from a gallows like frame with a large wooden stick with a paddle at the end (the knur).

A sports day at the Rochdale Cricket Club in the 1920s. The skyline is simply unrecognisable.

A local sporting tragedy. So many people wanted to watch Salford play Wigan in the Cup semi-final at the Athletic Grounds, in 1939 that every vantage point was taken. One person was killed and 14 injured when the grandstand collapsed. (Clifford C.Ashton)

In September 1935, fire destroyed the Hornets' main grandstand. (Clifford C.Ashton)

This is the 1922 Rochdale Hornets team which won the Northern Union Cup, beating Hull 10-9 in the final at Headingley. The attendance, a staggering 35,000, was the highest for a professional game to that date. Moreover, 40,000 people greeted the team on their triumphal return to Rochdale.

Meanwhile a change of codes. At Spotland, the home of Rochdale FC, Walter Birch (far right) is one of the players pictured training in the 1940s.

Here Walter Birch imparts his wisdom to young students of the beautiful game.

An appreciative home crowd at Spotland in October 1973. Not that there was much to cheer about that season, 'Dale being relegated to Division Four with only 21 points.

Social life has undergone radical changes over the last 100 years. Some traditional festivals and pastimes have disappeared only to re-appear recently in revivals like the Rochdale Rushcart procession which was revived in 1986. Borne on decorated carts, rushes were traditionally taken to strew on the floor of local churches. When Rochdale celebrated its Municipal Jubilee in 1906, one of the major attractions was the rushcart (pictured here). But even this was a revival. The coming of the railways and the provision of cheap excursions in the 1860s provided alternative entertainment for local people at holiday time and rushbearing festivals declined as a consequence.

Victorian sentimentality by the bucket load. This postcard from the 1890s juxtaposed poor local children and poet Edwin Waugh's dialect plea to straying fathers.

Not mushy peas, but the traditional black variety. A stall at a travelling fair in Milnrow at the turn of the century.

Bold Slasher and the King slug it out whilst the Doctor and Dirty Bet look on. The Easter Pace Egg play in Rochdale in the 1930s.

A more refined and respectable version of the Pace Egg ('Pace' as in the Easter Passion) as performed by the pupils of Rochdale Secondary School in 1938.

And still they battle on. The Wardle Pace Egg play outside the Globe Inn in 1964. (Clifford C. Ashton)

Rochdale wouldn't be Rochdale without the brass bands. Marching through Smithy Bridge in 1952.

The Milnrow Prize Band on Dale Street, Milnrow, in 1961.

Scouts march down Drake Street in 1968.

More music. In 1961 the Saints Jazz Band played at Rochdale Art Gallery. Jazz was revived in the building in 1995 courtesy of the Rochdale Jazz and Blues Club.

In the 1950s and 1960s there was the massively popular Miss Rochdale contest. It's November 1959, and congratulations to Jean Bowker, Miss Rochdale 1959-60.

Behind the scenes, a hairdressing contest was part of the build up to the 1961 Miss Rochdale contest.

If (in 1957) you applauded really loudly at the start of the Miss Rochdale Ball at the Town Hall...

...you got to see Shirley Bassey.

Eyes down. Mecca Bingo crowd in September 1961.

The sixties brought new forms of entertainment. Here is bingo at the Carlton in 1961.

The Young Socialists get ready to boogie on down at the Carlton in 1963.

In April 1964, the Rolling Stones were due to appear at Rochdale's Cubi-Klub in Slack Street. Over 800 packed the club and police had to struggle to hold back 1,000 fans disappointed at not being able to get a ticket. Two of the Stones were smuggled in and hidden away in the manager's office, but the other three were reported delayed when their vehicle had a puncture at Knutsford. The situation threatened to grow out of control and there was some violence, with four youths arrested, while twenty youngsters had to be treated after fainting. The manager's appeal for calm fell on deaf ears and it was decided, for safety reasons, that the Stones should not appear. Our photograph shows a police inspector leading away two of the casualties. (Clifford C.Ashton)

The Weighvers' Seaport

And now a section entirely devoted to the Weighvers' Seaport, our own Blackpool, the one and only Hollingworth Lake. On Good Friday 1964, the young, the old, the proto-mods and rockers bused, walked and drove there in their thousands. (Clifford C.Ashton)

The lake was built as a feeder reservoir for the Rochdale Canal, but has long served other purposes. In Edwardian times, as now, they came to the Lake to watch.

They came to promenade.

They came to paddle.

They came to use the pleasure boats.

They came to skate when, as in 1912, the Lake froze over.

Another side of Hollingworth Lake is seen here. Among the visitors ride some of the thousands of soldiers stationed here in vast camps during World War One.

So Many Things To Do

Garden parties were enjoyed by young and old. Here, in 1959, a good time was had by all at the Orthopaedic Hospital, Scott House.

The cinema and dancing. Two great post-war leisure industries represented here on a single photograph. The Carlton Ballroom (top) and Palace Cinema, Great George Street, just after the war.

Rochdale's first static cinema, the Old Circus, just before closure in 1908 when it played host to 'Pringle's Animated Pictures'. As the Hippodrome, this old corrugated building hosted Gracie Fields' first stage performance.

At one time the Rochdale area supported 11 cinemas. The two most luxurious premises in Rochdale were the Rialto (later the Odeon), Drake Street, and the Regal (pictured here in 1956). Built in 1938, the Regal – later the ABC and later still the Cannon Cinema – finally succumbed in 1993 to the bingo virus. Rochdale now has no cinema.

The Rialto, on Drake Street, a truly luxurious picture palace which closed its doors as the Odeon in 1975.

Originally built as the Prince of Wales Theatre in 1867, the Theatre Royal, Manchester Road, provided live entertainment until (already under a financial cloud) it was destroyed by fire in November 1954.

For the thirsty, Rochdale provided a wide variety of pubs some in odd locations. Here, stately Clegg Hall, built in 1610 is pictured as the Hare and Hounds public house in or around 1860.

'The most remarkable place of refreshment in the kingdom,' it was billed. The Boat Inn, usually called Uncle Tom's Cabin, was a former canal barge with roof added and sides walled up. It stood near Belfield Hall and the cabin walls 'looked out on pretty, rustic gardens'. This photograph dates from 1908.

High up on the moors, on Rooley Moor to be precise, the Moorcock Inn once catered for the thirsts of quarry men. As the quarries declined so did the pub, until it closed in the mid-1920s. The building was destroyed in target practice during the last war.

The Orchard Inn, demolished and submerged beneath the waters of Watergrove Reservoir in 1935. (Harry O'Neill)

On the site of a previous pub, the birthplace of dialect writer Edwin Waugh, the Old Clock Face on the corner of Toad Lane and Lord Street disappeared in the 1970s town centre redevelopment.

No it wasn't always the Sandknockers. Originally, and more prosaically it was the Red Lion Hotel, pictured here in around 1900.

In 1963 it's still the Red Lion.
Ramsden's Stone Trough Ales,
on sale at the neighbouring
Bull's Head, have disappeared.
(Leonard Russell)

The popular Duke
of Wellington, on
Blackwater Street,
was another
victim of the
1970s town centre
redevelopment.

Cheers!

Personalities And Celebrities

Cyril Smith (now Sir Cyril, of course) is a name synonymous with Rochdale. He was elected to the council in 1952 and became Mayor (he is pictured here in that role) and Alderman in 1966. In 1972 he became Liberal MP in a by-election, received the MBE in 1966, was knighted in 1988 and became Deputy Lieutenant of Greater Manchester in 1991. He stood down from Parliament in 1992.

The 1957 by-election in Rochdale made history by being the first to be televised. The Liberal candidate was the writer and broadcaster Ludovic Kennedy (right) pictured here with his wife, film star Moira Shearer and (from left) Robin Day, Councillor C.H.Fearn and Joe Grimond. In spite of the fame and glamour, Kennedy lost.

Granada Television cameras were allowed into the Town Hall to film the election candidates. (Clifford C.Ashton)

Gracie Fields was born above this shop in Molesworth Street on 9 January 1898. Born Gracie Stansfield, the printer Mr Bryning chose the name 'Fields' when Gracie's mother went to him to print business cards for her daughter.

In December 1934, Gracie returned to Rochdale to visit friends and familiar haunts. She is pictured at Mrs Schofield's off-licence in Milkstone Road where a gill (half pint) of beer cost only five old pence! (Clifford C.Ashton)

In 1937, Gracie was granted the Freedom of the Borough. The first woman to receive this honour, she said afterwards, "This was the proudest, most wonderful day of my life."

Gracie dons a fireman's helmet to inspect the town's emergency telephone switchboard in 1937, watched by the Mayor, Councillor Charlie Crowder, and Mr Henry Howarth, Chief Constable.

In 1938, Gracie went to Buckingham Palace; the first female entertainer to receive the CBE.

In 1978, Gracie returned to Rochdale to open the new shopping precinct. It was a great occasion watched by thousands of people.

Crowds packed Yorkshire Street to catch a glimpse of Rochdale's great entertainer.

The multi-storey car park proved a good vantage point for those unable to get a good place on the streets.

Boxer Jock McAvoy, real name Joseph Bamford, was known as the 'Rochdale Thunderbolt'. Although born in Burnley, he lived in Rochdale from a youngster and began fighting in the 1920s. A British middleweight champion, he was denied the world crown when he beat the American champion in a non-title fight.

Jack Howarth, *Coronation Street's* Albert Tatlock, was a Rochdale lad; born in the town in 1896.

Another local celebrity was John Ellis, the public hangman. His most famous victim was the Irish leader Roger Casement. Ellis later gave demonstrations at fairground shows. (Hannah Haynes)

A proud day for local historian Harvey Kershaw and his wife as they visit Buckingham Palace for him to receive the MBE.

The great Lancashire dialect writer Edwin Waugh was another local son. His stories and verses, often in a sentimental vein, were hugely popular and his books sold in enormous quantities. He is pictured here, towards the end of his life, when he had retired to New Brighton.

Pictured with his grandson is Rochdale's greatest son, John Bright. A manufacturer who became President of the Board of Trade, his name and that of Richard Cobden are forever linked with the great age of reform.

Capturing Rochdale on canvas is local artist Walter Kershaw who earned particular fame from his giant murals on large walls and the gable ends of houses.

Labour luminary Herbert Morrison was married to a Rochdale lass in 1955. Here, he and his wife, Edith (next to him), are pictured at a dinner of the Business and Professional Women's Guild in 1960. Formerly Edith Meadowcroft, she used to live in St Alban's Street.

Visitors

Grim weather greeted Housing Minister Earl Jellicoe when he and his team toured the slums of Rochdale in 1961 to see something of the housing problems facing the council.

In 1962 the slum problem was still with us. Dr Charles Hill, then the Housing Minister but better known for his previous role as the TV Doctor, visited Sand Street, Smallbridge, where the back-to-back houses on the left still had tub closets.

In November 1960, the artist L.S.Lowry visited Rochdale Art Gallery to inspect an exhibition. He is seen here with Leo Solomon, Principal of the Art College, on the left.

General Booth, founder of the Salvation Army, was 77 when he visited Rochdale in 1906 as part of a motor tour which took him from Inverness to Plymouth. He spoke at the Town Hall to 2,000 guests while up to 20,000 waited in Town Hall Square to see him.

Celebrations

A giant maypole was at the heart of the celebrations of the Silver Jubilee of King George V and Queen Mary.

The Silver Jubilee celebrations included ox-roasting on the Cattle Market.

In 1905, Falinge Park was opened with much civic splendour by Samuel Turner and Henry Fishwick.

Street parties have always been a great way of celebrating special occasions. Clover Hall Crescent celebrated VE Day in 1945 with this splendid one. (Eddie Clancy)

Clover Hall Crescent celebrated again for the Coronation in 1953. (Eddie Clancy)

This Milnrow shop was one of many to put out the bunting for a local Cycle Parade around the turn of the century.

James Wild's plumber's shop in Yorkshire Street is almost buried under decorations to celebrate the Rochdale Infirmary Gala held at Heybrook. The gala was an important means of funding the hospital.

The Hippodrome Theatre was bedecked to welcome royal visitors to Rochdale.

Mill girls never missed a chance to celebrate. Here the ring room section at Dunlop Mills is decked out for one royal occasion. (Mrs A.J.Whitworth)

The Coronation of King George VI was being celebrated on this occasion. (Mrs J. Travis)

Eclipse Mill celebrating the Coronation in 1953.

A large crowd turned out to watch the celebrations of Rochdale Police centenary in 1957.

At the Silver Jubilee celebrations in May 1935, this 'Feu de Joie' by the Lancashire Fusiliers was a memorable highlight. Each soldier fired his weapon in rapid succession to create what was described as an 'incredible sound'. The scene is the Esplanade, with the old police offices and the Theatre Royal on the right and the former library (soon to be Rochdale's Heritage Centre) on the left. (Clifford C.Ashton)

Chief Constable Henry Howarth, complete with sword, leads the police parade in celebration of the Silver Jubilee of King George V and Queen Mary. It is said that he helped design his splendid uniform. Described as 'a bit of a martinet and a stickler for rules', it was also acknowledged that he was very effective in policing the town. (Clifford C. Ashton)

A 'royal' occasion in 1914 for this young queen at the Rochdale Parish Church pageant.

Floats like this were always part of the carnival fun. This is at Kirkholt Carnival in 1962.

Processions

Whitsuntide was the time when churches 'walked'. The processions were hundreds strong and attracted many more spectators. Here is the scene in Blackwater Street, in 1950. (Clifford C.Ashton)

Cyril Smith, can just be seen (centre) in this procession by Rochdale Unitarian Church.

The procession at Holy Family RC Church in Kirkholt in 1959.

A scene from the procession at Smallbridge in 1961.

The Queen at Littleborough Parish Church in 1962.

The Church of the Good Shepherd walk in 1969.

Churches

St Chad's the parish church of Rochdale, before the tower was heightened.

This scene shows St Chad's with its present tower around 1920. The buildings are Leyland Chambers and the old corn mill.

Local Methodists built the magnificent and spacious – it has 1,600 seats – Champness mission hall in 1925. Thomas Champness after whom it is named was born in Essex in 1832 and went on to become a famous African missionary and founder of a college for training lay preachers and evangelists. There was controversy in 1977 when the notorious Sex Pistols pop group were booked to play here. But councillors decided to ban the event and the group received a £1,200 pay off.

Trinity Methodist Church at Lowerplace celebrated its centenary in 1929.

The horse-drawn Wesleyan Home Mission toured the area. Here it is pictured outside the chapel at Wardle.

St James' Church, Wardleworth, has changed little itself, although it is now used by the town's strong Ukrainian community rather than the Church of England. Its surroundings, though, are unrecognisable. Now it stands marooned in the centre of a busy roundabout.

This was the sad scene at Lanehead in August 1959, when the chapel opened its doors for the last time.

But there were happier times for the town's Mormons. This picture, taken in June 1961, shows the cutting of the first sod for the foundation of their new church.

War And Remembrance

The first parade of Volunteer Training Corps makes an impressive sight in Town Hall Square in October 1914.

The Manchester Territorials camped at Hollingworth Lake for training during World War One.

148

A military funeral in the grounds of Birch Hill Hospital during World War One.

Women at Tweedale and Smalley packing shells for use in World War One. (Mrs L.Keegan)

A huge parade, pictured here at the junction of Manchester Road and Drake Street, marked the declaration of peace in 1918.

On to World War Two and bomb damage at Holborn Street, Sudden, in 1941.

Bomb damage at Sudden in October 1941.

The Auxiliary Fire Service in action in 1943.

Evacuees wait on Rochdale Station for the train to take them to their new homes in Bacup.

Women and children dig for victory on a Rochdale allotment.

Fields became allotments, to boost food production. This picture, taken in 1941, shows the turf being removed at the start of the process.

This was the ARP control centre during World War Two.

The Rescue Party field kitchen in the Civil Defence parade in 1941.

A gloomy scene as Rochdale remembered its war dead in 1958.

This was Remembrance Sunday at Balderstone in 1961.

Doom And Disaster

Fires were a regular feature of cotton town life. Oil from the cotton, which is highly flammable, would permeate the whole building and once a fire was established it was very hard to bring under control. This picture shows Coal Bank Mill at Norden, destroyed by fire in March 1916.

A large crowd gathered to watch fire destroy the Gale Printworks.

This picture shows the dramatic scene when the Roch Valley Viaduct, on the Rochdale to Bacup line, was being demolished. Possibly the contractor used too much explosive, possibly there was a fault in the brickwork, but when arches over the river were felled the one across Entwisle Road, still open to traffic, came down too. People had to run for their lives, but amazingly no one was hurt. More than 2,000 people were evacuated from their homes before the arches were finally dealt with some days later.

This blaze at Clover Mill in June 1952, showed just how terrifying a mill fire could be. The blaze was caused when a workman using a blowtorch accidentally set fire to cotton in the basement. There was no sprinkler system in this part of the building but, even so, the firm's own firemen thought that they had extinguished the fire. But the flames were only dormant. Later smoke started to pour out of the bales of cotton and it was clear the matter had got out of rcontrol. By the time the regular Fire Brigade had been called the fire had taken too great a hold. The building was enveloped in smoke as the fire made its way up the building floor by floor. Eyewitnesses then saw the building which had previously been shrouded in smoke burst into the biggest flames imaginable. It was possibly the town's most dramatic blaze of all time and the blowtorch was later described in newspapers as 'the most expensive blowtorch in the world'.

One of Rochdale's most memorable blazes was when the Theatre Royal burned down in November 1954. (Clifford C.Ashton)

This was the dramatic scene in March 1969, when there was a blaze at the College of Art. (Clifford C.Ashton)

This was what
Clover Mill
interior looked like
after the fire of
June 1952. (Clifford
C.Ashton)

In April 1961, the
rubber works at Norden
suffered this disastrous
blaze. Two men in the
mill at the time had to
run for their lives.

These two photographs show the extent of damage at the giant Woolworth warehouse at Castleton after a disastrous fire, causing £4m of damage, in 1971. The building was formerly the Tweedale and Smalley works. (Clifford C. Ashton)

This scene from the air shows the giant warehouse rebuilt. (Clifford C.Ashton)

This was the scene facing motorists at Shawforth in 1963 when a mill collapsed across the road. (Clifford C.Ashton)

Robinson's Garage at Ramsay Street after a freak storm in August 1962, caused a stone supporting wall to be washed away by floodwater.

A freak wind in February 1976, caused the front wall of the Chinese restaurant at the corner of Lord Street and Newgate to collapse. Amazingly the tables inside were left totally intact. (Clifford C.Ashton)

Local Services

Not the most pleasant of jobs! These corporation workers had the job of collecting the night soil from the poorer parts of town, like these lodgings in Lord Street.

Earlier the task was undertaken using horse-drawn transport, pictured here in George Street.

Who better to make a presentation at Electric House in Smith Street, where the town's municipal electricity services were run from, than Rochdale's very own stage and screen star Gracie Fields?

The town's fire service on exercise at Hollingworth Lake. (Clifford C.Ashton)

Rochdale Town Council meet in the splendour of the Town Hall in March 1948. The room is now the Reception Room; the council sits in the former Police Court.

PC John Tyler, of Rochdale Borough Police, makes a call from a police phone in 1957.

At the other end of the phone could have been Audrey Bulcock, pictured at the police telephone switchboard in 1953.

Local youngsters listen attentively to a lesson in the public library.

Not the cavalry, but the massed horse flesh of Rochdale's Cleansing Department at the turn of the century.

There's nothing new about recycling as this cart load of by-products produced by the Cleansing Department shows.

'Waste not want not' was the motto during World War Two when this poster urged householders to keep a separate box of bones.

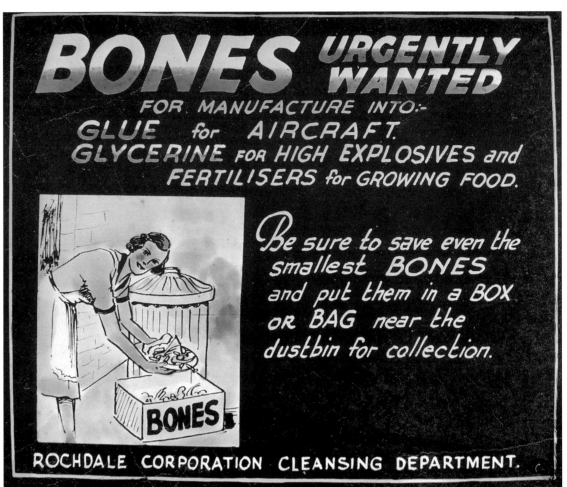

The scene at the corporation tip at Waithlands where an overhead pulley system was used to move the waste.

A street cleaning vehicle goes past John Bright's statue in the square.

At Rochdale Infirmary the matron's room was a scene of pre-war elegance.

The nurses' room at the Infirmary in 1965.

This new ambulance station was Wardle's pride and joy in February 1960.

Around The District

A tram rumbles down Market Street, Whitworth.

Clog-wearing children greet this tram outside the Dog and Partridge in Market Street. (Whitworth Museum)

The Whit Friday procession goes along Market Street. The picture was taken about 1910.

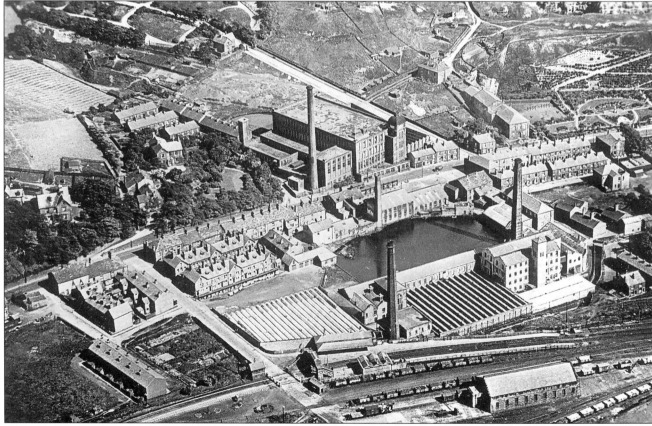

This aerial shot of Facit, taken in the 1920s, shows the cemetery in the background and bustling rail line in the foreground. (Whitworth Museum)

Whitworth has always had a proud reputation for cycling. The Whitworth Wheelers were well-known. Less famous, perhaps, was the Rossendale Tricycle Club shown here contesting the one mile race at Whitworth Track in July 1898. (Whitworth Museum)

Crowds gathered to witness the laying of the foundation stone at Lloyd Street School. (Whitworth Museum)

Jimmy Brandon and his band were resident at Whitworth Conservative Club in the 1930s. They were popular for miles around. (Whitworth Museum)

Hallfold and music are inseparable. Here, in 1950, the Hallfold Congregational Church Choir presents the *Mikado*. (Whitworth Museum)

The Riviera Swimming Pool at Norden was a popular venue on warm, sunny days such as the one on which this photograph was taken in 1935. The pool, now lost under new housing, was on the right-hand side of the road to Edenfield, on the hill above Greenbooth works. (Clifford C.Ashton)

Woodhouse Lane, Norden, seen from the air in this picture taken in 1938.

St Paul's Church and Moss Row in 1966. The row, since demolished, was regarded as the longest in the country.

Pictured in 1930 is the lost village of Greenbooth which now lies under the reservoir of the same name.

Another view of Greenbooth. The village had its own gasometer and a sort of central heating provided by the mill. The wife of the owner, Mrs Hutchinson, made it her business to inspect the villagers' front parlours for cleanliness.

A festive scene outside the White Hart Inn at Bamford.

Manchester Road, Castleton, looking towards the railway. The Bridge Inn on the corner of Queensway was still a property of the Bury Brewery Company which was later taken over by Blackburn brewers Thwaites.

Hare Hill Road, Littleborough, looking from Church Street. Craven's chemist shop is on the right and, in the distance, can be seen the imposing domed structure of the Co-op buildings which have since been demolished.

A fascinating view over Littleborough centre.

Littleborough Co-operative Society floats in the Cycle Parade of 1910.

A tram trundles along Church Street in the early years of this century.

Regulars of the Royal Exchange prepare for a trip in 1961.

Parading through the streets on Littleborough Chairman's Sunday in 1961.

This view of Summit a century ago shows a landscape almost worked to destruction.

A mechanical digger rumbles along Halifax Road in 1933 on its way to help in the construction of Watergrove Reservoir.

This picture shows Dearnley in 1902, looking substantially the same as today with the Methodist Church clearly to be seen. Littleborough is hidden in the industrial haze in the background.

A Rochdale tram makes its way along Dale Street, Milnrow.

Bridge Street, Milnrow, at the turn of the century.

Children pose in the street at the top of Buckley Hill Lane, Milnrow.

Newhey Road, Milnrow, in 1905, showing a clogger's shop on the left.

Milnrow rushcart prepares to set off on its tour of the town from the Plough Inn at the corner of Harbour Lane and Ladyhouse Lane. The pub was demolished in the 1960s.

Kettles were prizes at this event in bygone Wardle.

Wardle Fold with children grouped around the lamp-post.

Wardle Urban District Council offices.

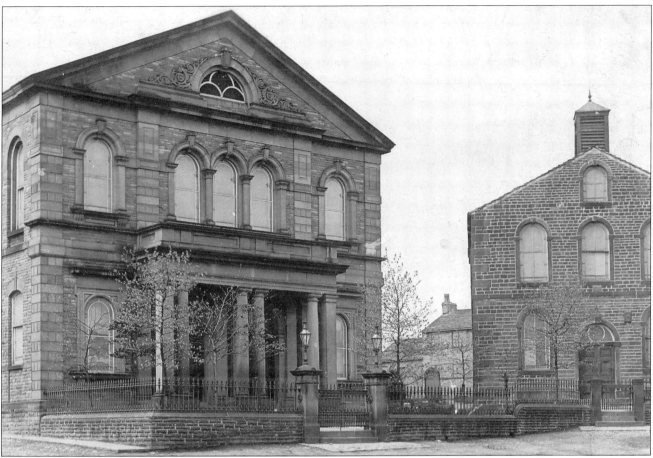

Wardle Chapel and Sunday school.

Sam Simpson is the driver of this fine-looking carriage pictured at Low Flat, Wardle.

A family poses proudly against this Wardle steam roller.

Wardle, like other local councils, had its annual Chairman's Sunday walk. This one was in 1962. In the background another familiar sight of the times, a 'What we want is Watneys' poster.

Construction work on the huge Watergrove Reservoir, which provided much-needed work for the area in 1935. (Clifford C.Ashton)

Another shot of the
Watergrove Reservoir,
construction work in 1935.
(Clifford C.Ashton)

Watergrove Mill in a ruined
state shortly before it
vanished, along with the rest
of Watergrove village, below
the waters of the reservoir.
(Clifford C.Ashton)